A W A K E

A W A K E

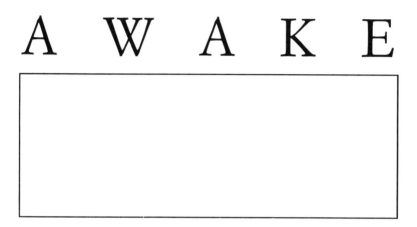

POEMS BY DORIANNE LAUX

FOREWORD BY PHILIP LEVINE

BOA EDITIONS, LTD., ROCHESTER, NEW YORK

ISBN: 0-918526-77-9 Paper

LC #: 89-82683
00 99 98 97 10 9 8 7 6

Publications by BOA Editions, Ltd.
are made possible with the assistance of grants from
the Literature Program of the New York State Council on the Arts
and the Literature Program of the National Endowment for the Arts,
as well as with financial assistance from private foundations,
corporations and individuals.
BOA Editions, Ltd. is a non-profit literary organization.

Cover Photograph: Nova Scotia interior © 1970 by Walker Evans
Reproduced with the permission of the Estate of Walker Evans
Cover Design: Daphne Poulin
BOA Logo: Mirko

Typesetting: Visual Studies Workshop
Manufacturing: McNaughton and Gunn

BOA Editions, Ltd.
A. Poulin, Jr., Founder and President (1976-1996)
Alexandra Northrop, Chair
260 East Ave.,
Rochester, NY 14604

CONTENTS

III

for Joel Rosen

FOREWORD

At a time when so much of our poetry seems obsessed with how it will stylishly say the little it has to say, it is exhilarating to discover a new poet who cares so much about the world we live in that she must search even the most hideous corners of it for their poetry. It is astonishing how much of the world Dorianne Laux can contain in her work. This is a poetry of risk: it will go to the very edge of extinction to find the hard facts that need to be sung, and one of the miracles of this collection is that every poem finds them, "like those flowers / you saw growing too close / to the tracks, bent and trembling / on the outskirts of Detroit." Those trembling flowers are like an emblem of all creatures and creations Ms. Laux takes to heart and writes of: they live far too close to the tracks because that is where they found life   If you're looking only for loveliness, you might as well look elsewhere, though there is plenty of loveliness here, for Dorianne Laux writes a beautifully sculptured, economical poem, and she has a stunning eye for the way the world actually looks, and when it is looking good, she is there to record it:

> I want to smell this rich soup, the air
> around me going dark, as stars press
> their simple shapes into the sky.
> I want to stay on the back porch
> while the world tilts
> toward sleep, until what I love
> misses me and calls me in.

This passage is from one of the most joyful poems in the collection, "On the Back Porch," a small domestic fable that captures the speaker's double nature as a mother and lover; it is also the final, summary poem of the second section of the book, which deals largely with the difficulties and joys of raising children. If you've read *Awake* from the first poem on, by the time you get here you will have traveled through many lives, for this is above all a book of lives, some of which are almost unbearably painful.

Milton wrote that he could not "praise a fugitive and cloistered virtue, unexercised and unbreathed, that never sallies out

8

and sees her adversary..." The poems in this book are unafraid to sally out; they go where we live, they find us at our best and our worst, they watch us suffer insult, injustice, incest, torture, and they do not turn away, for their burden is to accept and even to bless. In what is perhaps the central poem of the collection, "Quarter to Six," we have the remarkable image of two young women maddened and discarded in the wards of a public asylum. They do their best to help each other through their private hells, and when they have nothing else to share, they share the memories of the pain which brought them there. In the climactic scene they trade stories of their military fathers: "yours locking you in a closet for the days it took/—to chew ribbons of flesh from your fingers, and "mine, who worked/his ringed fingers inside me while the house/slept..." Before the poem ends, they meet again as adult and sane women, they hug and kiss, and one gives the other the magical gift of prophecy.

It is in our world, immersed in the grubby facts of our experience, that these poems retain a kind of innocence, a purity in their ability to look at each new day freshly and dare to hope it will bring its gifts. It is as though Ms. Laux decided to fuse the visions of Blake's Innocence and Experience in a single collection of poems. In a conventional sense these poems are not innocent; they seem unable to look away from life as it is lived, and their courage is their refusal not to see. No matter what grief they endure, they come back again and again, and their mission is not a resignation merely to suffer. No, Dorianne Laux's poems are sassy, pugnacious, and their voice is energized with whatever glory sustains life. Their innocence is in their faith that no matter what, life is worth having and worth transforming into poetry:

> Morning will come because it has to.
> You will open your eyes. The sun
> will flare and rise. Chisel the hills
> into shape. The sax player next door
> will lift his horn and pour
> music over the downturned Vs of rooftops,
> the tangled ivy, the shivering tree,
> giving it all back to us as he breathes:
> The garden. The hard blue sky. The sweet
> apple of light.

9

Without knowing it, Ms. Laux has described the effect of her own poetry on us.

It is easy to read these poems and not be aware of their artistry, because their subjects demand so much attention. Constantly rewarding the ear, *Awake* is a book written with enormous precision and beauty. It has such confidence in its authority, it overstates nothing. Sculptured, economical, tough, possessing a vision informed by experience and compassion, this is an astonishingly mature first book, the wisest I have read in years.

—Philip Levine

I

GHOSTS

It's midnight and a light rain falls.
I sit on the front stoop to smoke.
Across the street a lit window, filled
with a ladder on which a young man stands.
His head dips into the frame each time
he sinks his brush in the paint.

He's painting his kitchen white, patiently
covering the faded yellow with long strokes.
He leans into his work like a lover, risks
losing his balance, returns gracefully
to the precise middle of the step to dip
and start again.

A woman appears beneath his feet, borrows
paint, takes it onto her thin brush
like a tongue. Her sweater is the color
of tender lemons. This is the beginning
of their love, bare and simple
as that wet room.

My hip aches against the damp cement.
I take it inside, punch up a pillow
for it to nest in. I'm getting too old
to sit on the porch in the rain,
to stay up all night, watch morning
rise over rooftops.

Too old to dance
circles in dirty bars, a man's hands
laced at the small of my spine, pink
slingbacks hung from limp fingers. Love.
I'm too old for that, the foreign tongues
loose in my mouth, teeth that rang
my breasts by the nipples like soft bells.

I want it back. The red earrings and blue
slips. Lips alive with spit. Muscles
twisting like boat ropes in a hard wind.
Bellies for pillows. Not this ache in my hip.

I want the girl who cut through blue poolrooms
of smoke and golden beers, stepping out alone
into a summer fog to stand beneath a streetlamp's
amber halo, her blue palms cupped
around the flare of a match.

She could have had so many lives. Gone off
with a boy to Arizona, lived on a ranch
under waves of carved rock, her hands turned
the color of flat red sands. Could have said
yes to a woman with fingers tapered as candles,
or a man who slept in a canvas tepee, who pulled
her down on his mattress of grass where she made
herself as empty as the gutted fire.

                              Oklahoma.
I could be there now, spinning corn from dry cobs,
working fat tomatoes into mason jars.

The rain has stopped. For blocks the houses
drip like ticking clocks. I turn off lights
and feel my way to the bedroom, slip cold
toes between flowered sheets, nest my chest
into the back of a man who sleeps in fits,
his suits hung stiff in the closet, his racked
shoes tipped toward the ceiling.

This man loves me for my wit, my nerve,
for the way my long legs fall from hemmed skirts.
When he rolls his body against mine, I know
he feels someone else. There's no blame.
I love him, even as I remember a man with cane-
brown hands, palms pink as blossoms opening
over my breasts.

         And he holds me,
even with all those other fingers wrestling
inside me, even with all those other shoulders
wedged above his own like wings.

TWO PICTURES OF MY SISTER

If an ordinary person is silent,
this may be a tactical maneuver.
If a writer is silent, this is lying.
                    —*Jaroslav Seifert*

The pose is stolen from Monroe, struck
in the sun's floodlight, eyes lowered,
a long-stemmed plastic rose between her teeth.
My cast off bathing suit hangs
in folds over her ribs, straps
cinched, pinned at the back of her neck.
Barefoot on the hot cement, knock-kneed,
comical if it weren't for the graceful
angles of her arms, her flesh soft
against the chipped stucco.

The other picture is in my head.
It is years later.
It is in color.
Blond hair curls away from the planes of her face
like wood shavings.
She wears a lemon-yellow ruffled top, denim
cut-offs, her belly button squeezed to a slit
above the silver snap.
She stands against the hallway wall
while Dad shakes his belt in her face.
A strip of skin has been peeled
from her bare shoulder, there are snake
lines across her thighs, a perfect curl
around her long neck.
She looks through him
as if she could see behind his head.
She dares him.
Go on. Hit me again.

He lets the folded strap unravel to the floor.
Holds it by its tail. Bells the buckle
off her cheekbone.
She does not move or cry or even wince
as the welt blooms on her temple
like a flower opening frame by frame
in a nature film.
It lowers her eyelid with its violet petals
and as he walks away only her eyes
move, like the eyes of a portrait that follow you
around a museum room, her face
a stubborn moon that trails the car all night,
stays locked in the frame of the back window
no matter how many turns you take,
no matter how far you go.

AUGUSTA

for my mother
Frances Margarette Comeau

She is born in a white room
in winter in the short
light to a shout of birds, the sky
locked in ice. Found on a convent
doorstep, nuns' black hoods dip
like coal scuttles to her cry.
Fed potato milk, she thins
into adolescence, grows beans up poles
in a patch behind the chapel.

Piano practice. The oldest nun breaks
a switch from a branch, holds it
over the keys, rings
the twig off her knuckles until
the right note sounds.

Summer cracks the dirt road.
She sits on the rotting end
of the porch, smokes cigarettes
stolen from a visitor's purse.
Draws nipples on the sculpted cherubs.
Is beaten for this.
Is beaten for most things.

Night rolls her body over, thin cot
smells of piss and moldy ticking, the moon
peeling as she leaves, elbows sharp,
her new heels spike through snow.

Italian, he says, her dark hair
wasted in his hands. *No,* she whispers,
Algonquin, works with him to make
a single shape.

This is where I begin, as a fist
pounds the wall for quiet. As snow
breaks loose from the eaves.

I am not old enough to remember
the broom handle in his hands, her teeth
skipping kitchen tiles, blood
that spattered the bassinet to dotted swiss.

Winter can't hold her in. Her tracks
leave blue chains on the snow, a path
from his open door of yellow light.

In California she speaks French, sips
amber tea, ice chipping in a sweaty glass.
She meets the sailor who will become
my new father. He holds me to his chest.
She smiles. Her hand covers her mouth.

WHAT MY FATHER TOLD ME

Always I have done what was asked.
Melmac dishes stacked on rag towels.
The slack of a vacuum cleaner cord
wound around my hand. Laundry
hung on a line.
There is always much to do and I do it.
The iron resting in its frame, hot
in the shallow pan of summer
as the basins of his hands push
aside the book I am reading.
I do as I am told, hold his penis
like the garden hose, in this bedroom,
in that bathroom, over the toilet
or my bare stomach.
I do the chores, pull weeds out back,
finger stink-bug husks, snail carcasses,
pile dead grass in black bags. At night
his feet are safe on their pads, light
on the wall-to-wall as he takes
the hallway to my room.
His voice, the hiss of lawn sprinklers,
the wet hush of sweat in his hollows,
the mucus still damp
in the corners of my eyes as I wake.

Summer ends. Schoolwork doesn't suit me.
My fingers unaccustomed to the slimness
of a pen, the delicate touch it takes
to uncoil the mind.
History. A dateline pinned to the wall.

Beneath each president's face, a quotation.
Pictures of buffalo and wheatfields,
a wagon train circled for the night,
my hand raised to ask the question,
Where did the children sleep?

THE NURSE

My mother went to work each day
in a starched white dress, shoes
clamped to her feet like pale
mushrooms, two blue hearts pressed
into the sponge rubber soles.
When she came back home, her nylons
streaked with runs, a spatter
of blood across her bodice,
she sat at one end of the dinner table
and let us kids serve the spaghetti, sprinkle
the parmesan, cut the buttered loaf.
We poured black wine into the bell
of her glass as she unfastened
her burgundy hair, shook her head, and began.
And over the years we mastered it, how to listen
to stories of blocked intestines
while we twirled the pasta, of saws
teething cranium, drills boring holes in bone
as we crunched the crust of our sourdough,
carved the stems off our cauliflower.
We learned the importance of balance,
how an operation depends on
cooperation and a blend of skills,
the art of passing the salt
before it is asked for.
She taught us well, so that when Mary Ellen
ran the iron over her arm, no one wasted
a moment: My brother headed straight for the ice.
Our little sister uncapped the salve.

And I dialed the number under Ambulance,
my stomach turning to the smell
of singed skin, already planning the evening
meal, the raw fish thawing in its wrapper,
a perfect wedge of flesh.

THE TWINS

The only feature June and Jerry had in common
was their red hair, and their hands.
On Sundays they ran with sticks.
Hammered trashcans like banshees.
Wheeled past me through the backyard gate
to bounce their voices off the canyon walls
with those animal shrieks small larynxes make—
It was the summer I discovered
fool's gold in a tangle of manzanita.

We played those canyons like a deep song.
Stomped our brutal tunes into the dry dirt.
Yelled. Listened to our own voices return.
In the afternoons mothers fried fat potatoes
on the griddle, lured us home with the smell
of soup bones and split peas. Their hands—

the fingers webbed together
like the pink feet of ducks, attached
at the wrists to pairs of perfect freckled arms
that grew into swan white backs, punctuated
by shoulder blades: wing nubs
pinking in the sun.

My sun-browned hands were scaly and scratched
from playing hide-and-seek in the sagebrush.
Like a lizard I curled into the shade
of a low bush and hid, watching my heart
beat hard through my clothes, wondering
in the stillness and the shadows how
the blood flows, where the mind goes
when you're dead, why the simple grace
of the hand was marred by something as ugly
as the thumb. It was at night

that their hands got that way. I never asked
back then, but years later my mother told me
how their mother—a woman she said
was bony, beaten, spent her days
reading the Bible—once ran naked
into the street, singing hymns. It began
with the dirt ground into their small knees, or
a tear in the cloth near the pocket—
a hard spot to mend. Muttering "Cleanliness

is next to Godliness," she bathed them
together in the clawfoot tub, dragged them
down the hall by their blazing hair, their scalps
burning, their fingertips grasping at walls
sheer as the shale in the canyon bed. Then

as the last light bruised the sky, she
punished them for being dirty—took those hands,
white as dough and flecked with sweet
cinnamon spots, and held them
over the floor heater, until the miracle
happened, until the skin melted
into itself, until the hands rose up
red as their hair and glowed and the street
echoed with their screams, until at last
they were clean, and forgiven.

QUARTER TO SIX

and the house swept with the colors of dusk,
I set the table with plates and lace. In these minutes
left to myself, before the man and child scuff at the doorstep
and come in, I think of you and wonder what I would say
if I could write. Would I tell you how I avoid his eyes,
this man I've learned to live with, afraid
of what he doesn't know about me. That I've finished
a pack of cigarettes in one sitting, to ready myself
for dinner, when my hands will waver over a plate of fish
as my daughter grows up normal in the chair beside me. Missy,

this is what's become of the wedding you swore you'd come to
wearing black. That was in 1970 as we sat on the bleached
floor of the sanitarium sharing a cigarette you'd won
in a game of pool. You said even school was better
than this ward, where they placed the old men
in their draped pants, the housewives screaming in loud
flowered shifts as they clung to the doors that lined the halls.
When we ate our dinner of fish and boiled potatoes,
it was you who nudged me under the table
as the thin man in striped pajamas climbed
the chair beside me in his bare feet, his pink-tinged urine
making soup of my leftovers. With my eyes locked on yours,
I watched you keep eating. So I lifted my fork
to my open mouth, jello quivering green
against the tines, and while I trusted you and chewed
on nothing, he leapt into the arms of the night nurse
and bit open the side of her face. You had been there

longer, knew the ropes, how to take the sugar-coated pill
and slip it into the side pocket in your mouth, pretend
to swallow it down in drowsy gulps while
the white-frocked nurse eyed the clockface above our heads.
You tapped messages into the wall while I wept, struggling
to remember the code, snuck in after bedcount
with cigarettes, blew the blue smoke through barred windows.
We traded stories, our military fathers:
yours locking you in a closet for the days it took
to chew ribbons of flesh from your fingers, a coat
pulled over your head; mine, who worked
his ringed fingers inside me while the house
slept, my face pressed to the pillow, my fists
knotted into the sheets. Some nights

I can't eat. The dining room fills
with their chatter, my hand stuffed with the glint
of a fork and the safety of butter knives
quiet at the sides of our plates. If I could write you now,
I'd tell you I wonder how long I can go on with this careful
pouring of the wine from the bottle, straining to catch it
in the fragile glass. Tearing open my bread, I see

the scar, stitches laced up the root of your arm, the flesh messy
where you grabbed at it with the broken glass of an ashtray.
That was the third time. And later you laughed
when they twisted you into the white strapped jacket
demanding you vomit the pills. I imagined you
in the harsh light of a bare bulb where you took
the needle without flinching, retched
when the ipecac hit you, your body shelved over
the toilet and no one to hold the hair
from your face. I don't know

where your hands are now, the fingers that filled my mouth
those nights you tongued me open in the broken light
that fell through chicken-wired windows. The intern
found us and wrenched us apart, the half-moon of your breast
exposed as you spit on him. "Now you're going to get it,"
he hissed through his teeth and you screamed "Get what?"
As if there was anything anyone could give you.
If I could write you now, I'd tell you

I still see your face, bone-white as my china
above the black velvet cape you wore to my wedding
twelve years ago, the hem of your black crepe skirt
brushing up the dirty rice in swirls
as you swept down the reception line to kiss me.
"Now you're going to get it," you whispered,
cupping my cheek in your hand.

THE TOOTH FAIRY

They brushed a quarter with glue
and glitter, slipped in on bare
feet, and without waking me
painted rows of delicate gold
footprints on my sheets with a love
so quiet, I still can't hear it.

My mother must have been
a beauty then, sitting
at the kitchen table with him,
a warm breeze lifting her
embroidered curtains, waiting
for me to fall asleep.

It's harder to believe
the years that followed, the palms
curled into fists, a floor
of broken dishes, her chainsmoking
through long silences, him
punching holes in his walls.

I can still remember her print
dresses, his checkered Taxi, the day
I found her in the closet
with a paring knife, the night
he kicked my sister in the ribs.

He lives alone in Oregon now, dying
slowly of a rare bone disease.
His face stippled gray, his ankles
clotted beneath wool socks.

She's a nurse on the graveyard shift.
Comes home mornings and calls me.
Drinks her dark beer and goes to bed.

And I still wonder how they did it, slipped
that quarter under my pillow, made those
perfect footprints...

Whenever I visit her, I ask again.
"I don't know," she says, rocking, closing
her eyes. "We were as surprised as you."

SKIPPING STONES

I was thirteen the summer the family went to visit
Grandma Laux in Oregon. We passed her place
three times before we finally saw her, running
down the middle of the street in her house slippers
screaming, "This is it. Park the damn thing."
She was still alone at sixty-five and the neighbors
thought she was crazy, sitting at the attic
window, her angora cat slopped over the sill,
typing her autobiography.

I learned to skip stones at Miller's Pond. My cousin
taught me how to sift the low slope of bedrock
and choose only the flattest, smoothest stones.
His loose arm shot over the shallow part of the pond
a million times that summer. At dusk I watched
his silhouette ripple, his curved wrist scythe the air
between the water and the scooped out moon.

The last day of that vacation I waited while he hit
every drugstore on the outskirts of town.
He finally showed up, with a thin smile and a rubber.
His face was flushed with the heat, I was nervous,
but when he opened the door to his basement bedroom,
it was cool and smelled of wood shavings
and Testor paints. He kept his pants on, just in case,
and when I lifted my best dress carefully,
not to wrinkle it, he giggled and I closed my eyes.

I will always wonder how we didn't hear
the car or the footsteps on the creaking stairs.
I do know that the look on my father's face
and the beating that came after
ruined any ideas I had about romance.

Eighteen years and as many lovers later, you and I
stand on the edge of Coniston Water, skipping stones.
Every day of this vacation I have been moody, distant,
every night we've come into a new town too late
and have struggled with our bags up three flights
of stairs to the small attic flats where you
fall on the bed, exhausted, and I set up my portable
typewriter, rinse out my angora sweater
and hang it over the window sill to dry.

When the only sound is the skipping of stones, I tell you
I'm beginning to like it, these small one-window rooms
with a view. You had given up on romance until now,
when you point to the ringed water and tell me
this is what your heart does every time I touch you.

It would be simple, in the moonlight, to say nothing
and reach for your hand. Instead I ask you to show me
again how to lob a stone into the middle of the lake
so that it sounds like stabbing a watermelon.

WHEN I WAS BORN

the world was filled with fat hands,
pillows, my own earlobes. Too full

to eat, I grabbed at feet, pink toes
sucked into a single idea, blue milk,

gutters on plastic bibs, the bars
of light banging into my crib.

One day there was a new bed,
the wholeness of a room saved

in square chunks like an old puzzle.
I was closer to the floor, farther

from the ceiling, and all the window
showed was sky. At night sockets

hissed, the moon lit, my hot body
turning between cool white sheets.

The world began to make patterns,
designs, dishes stacked by size, cars

in the driveway. Down for Off. Up
for On. Socks and underwear in the top

drawer. It all made sense, rabbits
in holes, fences erect, then the wind

came unpinned, began whipping the dust.
I crawled under a bush, found a lizard

crushed, eyes spit out on either side
and twitching in the dirt, the tail

still alive. All the walk home I watched
the sky, waited for the world to take me

by surprise, reach up and twist its arms
around my chest, squeeze out my eyes.

But what I saw was a bluejay lift
from a wire, her body hovering on

nothing but air, and fling one strong note
as she stretched her wings to disappear

in the arms of a tree. For years that day
followed me, went to school in my lunchbag,

flattened itself into my books, screeched
green chalkboards with heat-white claws,

crawled under bathroom doors.
And when it wouldn't let go, I kicked

the boys on the stairs, spit in gutters
and stepped on cracks, ran home

to my room, stripped to my socks, turned
up the radio, shut out the sky.

Then, spreading my arms, I closed my eyes
and taught myself to dance.

—for Patricia

AWAKE

Except for the rise and fall of a thin sheet
draped across your chest, you could be dead.
Your hair curled into the pillow.
Arms flung wide. The moon fills our window
and I stand in a white
rectangle of light. Hands crossed
over empty breasts. In an hour
the moon will lower itself. In the backyard
the dog will bark, dig up his bone
near the redwood fence. If we could have had
children, or religion, maybe sleep
wouldn't feel like death, like shovel heads
packing the black earth down.
Morning will come because it has to.
You will open your eyes. The sun
will flare and rise. Chisel the hills
into shape. The sax player next door
will lift his horn and pour
music over the downturned Vs of rooftops,
the tangled ivy, the shivering tree,
giving it all back to us as he breathes:
The garden. The hard blue sky. The sweet
apple of light.

ON THE RIVER

Last night we slept in the old van, our backs
flat on a wood riser some other couple built
56,000 miles ago. My daughter slept in her tent
with a friend, the canvas held down with halves
of broken rock. It was for her that we'd traveled
this far, had camped by the river, would work
to salvage whatever remained.
After making love, I opened the curtains, watched
The Plough slide through sycamore branches.
Cold air seeped through doors that no longer
closed flush, the same glossy chill
that pressed up our legs that afternoon
as we swayed over riverbed rocks, salted
with turquoise or struck through
with rippled ribbons of quartz. The children
were farther down the bank, beyond the failure
of our voices, their ankles lost
in a wilderness of shiners, gnats floating
in gold follicles of light around their heads.
We waved, then bent to the river, invaded
its tight skin with our fingers, raised clouds
of silt as we scavenged for something to carry
home, a rock so perfect it would startle us
awake in the nights to follow, a smooth stone
that would deny the cars cranking by
on the cliffside road, the broken bottle
sunk deep in the weeds, a skeet shooter's rifle
shifting in the distance, one shot—then two.

RETURN

My daughter, ten and brown—another summer
in Arizona with her father—steps
nonchalantly down the ramp as planes
unfurl their ghostly plumes of smoke.
I had forgotten how his legs, dark
and lean as hers, once strode toward me
across a stretch of hammered sand.
And her shoulders, sloped like his, a cotton
blouse scooped so low I can see
her collar bones arched gracefully
as wings, the cruel dip
in the hollow of her throat. And my throat
closes when she smiles, her bangs
blown into a fan around her face, hair
blond as the pampas grass that once waved
wild behind our fence. Whatever held us
together then is broken, dishes
in pieces on the floor, his dead
cigarettes crushed one after another
into the rail of the porch.
Now she opens her arms as he
used to, against a backdrop of blue sky,
so wide I worry she'll float up on these
gusts of clutching wind and disappear,
like a half-remembered dream, into
the perilous future, into the white
heart of the sun.

GIRL IN THE DOORWAY

She is twelve now, the door to her room
closed, telephone cord trailing the hallway
in tight curls. I stand at the dryer, listening
through the thin wall between us, her voice
rising and falling as she describes her new life.
Static flies in brief blue stars from her socks,
her hairbrush in the morning. Her silver braces
shine inside the velvet case of her mouth.
Her grades rise and fall, her friends call
or they don't, her dog chews her new shoes
to a canvas pulp. Some days she opens her door
and musk rises from the long crease in her bed,
fills the dim hall. She grabs a denim coat
and drags the floor. Dust swirls in gold eddies
behind her. She walks through the house, a goddess,
each window pulsing with summer. Outside,
the boys wait for her teeth to straighten.
They have a vibrant patience.
When she steps onto the front porch, sun shimmies
through the tips of her hair, the V of her legs,
fans out like wings under her arms
as she raises them and waves. Goodbye, Goodbye.
Then she turns to go, folds up
all that light in her arms like a blanket
and takes it with her.

BREAK

We put the puzzle together piece
by piece, loving how one curved
notch fits so sweetly with another.
A yellow smudge becomes
the brush of a broom, and two blue arms
fill in the last of the sky.
We patch together porch swings and autumn
trees, matching gold to gold. We hold
the eyes of deer in our palms, a pair
of brown shoes. We do this as the child
circles her room, impatient
with her blossoming, tired
of the neat house, the made bed,
the good food. We let her brood
as we shuffle through the pieces,
setting each one into place with a satisfied
tap, our backs turned for a few hours
to a world that is crumbling, a sky
that is falling, the pieces
we are required to return to.

BIRD

For days now a red-breasted bird
has been trying to break in.
She tests a low branch, violet blossoms
swaying beside her, leaps into the air and flies
straight at my window, beak and breast
held back, claws raking the pane.
Maybe she lunges for the tree she sees
reflected in the glass, but I'm only guessing.
I watch until she gives up and swoops off.
I wait for her return, the familiar
click, swoosh, thump of her. I sip cold coffee
and scan the room, trying to see it new,
through the eyes of a bird. Nothing has changed.
Books piled in a corner, coats hooked
over chair backs, paper plates, a cup
half-filled with sour milk.
The children are in school. The man is at work.
I'm alone with dead roses in a jam jar.
What do I have that she could want enough
to risk such failure, again and again?

42

ON THE BACK PORCH

The cat calls for her dinner.
On the porch I bend and pour
brown soy stars into her bowl,
stroke her dark fur.
It's not quite night.
Pinpricks of light in the eastern sky.
Above my neighbor's roof, a transparent
moon, a pink rag of cloud.
Inside my house are those who love me.
My daughter dusts biscuit dough.
And there's a man who will lift my hair
in his hands, brush it
until it throws sparks.
Everything is just as I've left it.
Dinner simmers on the stove.
Glass bowls wait to be filled
with gold broth. Sprigs of parsley
on the cutting board.
I want to smell this rich soup, the air
around me going dark, as stars press
their simple shapes into the sky.
I want to stay on the back porch
while the world tilts
toward sleep, until what I love
misses me, and calls me in.

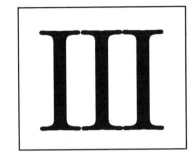

CROSS COUNTRY

When the train stops to fuel up,
they have to shut the power down.
You have to use the bathroom
in the dark, have to eye the hole
as the door slides closed, clicks
into the lock. If you're a woman,
you have to squat near where you think
the hole still is, not daring to touch
to make sure. You hover above a rising warmth
and force yourself to pee, not knowing, hoping
your aim is true. When you come out,
a row of kids, their filthy ears
pressed to the metal wall, have been listening,
are still giggling deep in their throats,
their mothers asleep in the hard yellow seats,
nothing left to see but backyards, stacked
car parts, miles of cramped city.
You don't want to look back
but you do, to where they crowd the open door,
the train windows' dirty light seeping in
around their skinny necks. They creep
to the spot you just left
to take in the wild scent: a raw mix
of sweat, excrement and disinfectant.
"Smell it," they whisper to each other,
bumping shoulders gently in the dark,
their stringy hair and heavy heads
hung forward, toward something they know
they should know, drooped with longing
toward what reminds them of a soft mound
of dirt, the earth, like those flowers
you saw growing too close
to the tracks, bent and trembling
on the outskirts of Detroit.

WATER STREET BRIDGE

On the turnpike to Augusta, birches
white between fat pines, rivers
whisper their Indian names. Brick
smokestacks still drum black clouds
above the hospital where my mother lay,
braced for the small head to crown
slowly between her thighs.

It was January. Basement pipes
must have moaned and bled rust
as she pushed, gusts of ochre steam
rolling below her through the dark.
She must have been cold, her knuckles
white on the handrails. Snow settling
in powdery drifts on the sill.

Thirty-five years later
I drive over this bridge and wonder
which room was hers.
I want to stop and go in, touch
the bed where she slept, find
what my eyes first opened and closed on
in this foreign light.

I've walked to the edge of the Kennebec River
to see what she must have seen.
Waking alone. My body
so new in her arms. There are the reeds

stabbed up through the silver
skin of the river, the bridge
criss-crossed with steel ropes,
a lone truck with mud on its tires
threading its way to Hollowell.

THAW

I have come North in winter to watch
a pond outside my window rise
and freeze over, to feel this happen
as I sleep, to wait patiently as ice
inches toward the small falls, to see
how the cold makes a sluggish
chore of it, the whole system shut down
between two chinks of time, frozen finally
in the shape of falling.

I have come to walk across that pond
in its hibernation, the sad fish,
the pond's misted breath sealed
tight beneath its layered self,
to step as lightly as gravity allows
onto its thickening skin, the raised
proud flesh of it, to become stupid
with bravery and faith, no longer testing
the center's slick belly but leaping,
gliding on ice.

I have come here to accomplish this,
to lean into the wind and learn, to stand
without falling between water and sky,
to know for the first time the simple power
of cold, how even the earth's chilled blood
will never fail me.

CHINA

From behind he looks like a man
I once loved, that hangdog slouch
to his jeans, a sweater vest, his neck
thick-veined as a horse cock, a halo
of chopped curls.

He orders coffee and searches
his pockets, first in front, then
from behind, a long finger sliding
into the slitted denim the way that man
slipped his thumb into me one summer
as we lay after love, our freckled
bodies two pale starfish on the sheets.

Semen leaked and pooled in his palm
as he moved his thumb slowly, not
to excite me, just to affirm
he'd been there.

I have loved other men since, taken
them into my mouth like a warm vowel,
lain beneath them and watched their irises
float like small worlds in their open eyes.

But this man pressed his thumb
toward the tail of my spine
as if he were entering
China, or a ripe papaya,
so that now
when I think of love
I think of this.

THE LAUNDROMAT

My clothes somersault in the dryer. At thirty
I float in and out of a new kind of horniness,
the kind where you get off on words and gestures;
long talks about art are foreplay, the climax
is watching a man eat a Napoleon while he drives.
Across from me a fifty year old matron folds clothes,
her eyes focused on the nipples of a young man in
silk jogging shorts. He looks up, catching her.
She giggles and blurts out, "Hot, isn't it?"
A man on my right eyes the line of my shorts, waiting
for me to bend over. I do. An act of animal kindness.
A long black jogger swings in off the street to
splash his face in the sink and I watch the room
become a sweet humid jungle. We crowd around
the Amazon at the watering hole, twitching our noses
like wildebeests or buffalo, snorting, rooting out
mates in the heat. I want to hump every moving thing
in this place. I want to lie down in the dry dung
and dust and twist to scratch my back. I want to
stretch and prowl and grow lazy in the shade. I want
to have a slew of cubs. "Do you have change for
a quarter?" he asks, scratching the inside of his thigh.
Back in the laundromat my socks are sticking to my
sheets. Caught in the crackle of static electricity,
I fold my underwear. I notice the honey-colored
stains in each silk crotch. Odd-shaped, like dreams,
I make my panties into neat squares and drop them,
smiling, into the wicker basket.

ADAM'S DAD TEACHES
THE KIDS TO PLAY BALL

Dad stands on the mound preaching
fairness and order. Adam squirms
on the grassy sidelines and cries.
He doesn't want to learn patience,
his chin slick with tears
and bright snot, gold hair chopped
into a perfect cap on his head.
Adam's brother Moses, dark-haired,
older, runs the park's imaginary bases—
his tall sister Melissa, equipped
with a face mask, a mitt that spans
the width of her chest, catches
missed balls behind her brother's back.
Adam screams. Calls them names. Falls
on the grass, kicks clumps into the air
until dad picks him up, plants his
feet on the ground, sticks the bat
between his short fingers, instructs
his youngest in the grip and swing
that sends winning Spauldings spinning
into blue American skies. Adam's dad
shields his eyes and pitches and pitches.
Adam misses and misses, his sister bored
stiff in his stubby shadow, his brother
shifting from foot to foot. Adam sinks
his bare toes into the dirt, flattens
grass with the blunt end of the bat
as dad winds up for the pitch
with a promise: *This is your last chance.*

Then the miracle happens: Adam's bat
cracks like an apple—the ball slung
toward the sun—and as Moses, Melissa
and dad follow its arc with unbelieving
eyes, Adam runs and runs into the beginning
of his life, a rough circle that ends
in a slide between dad's spread legs, huge
biceps that strain at the flared white
cuffs of his shirt—his father a God
or a muscular angel who digs his heels
into the earth as he sings against
the low-domed sky the one song he knows:
He's safe. Safe.
He's home.

THE CHILDREN'S TRAIN

As the train approaches the tunnel, the kids
gear up to scream. They pull the darkening
air into their lungs, keep their eyes wide.
The light withdraws in stages, shrinks away
from the floor, the backsides of seats, slips
down the curved ceiling before leaping
like spooked deer through the open windows.
The brave ones squeal into each other's
disappearing faces, poke and pinch their younger
sister's naked knees, but when even the boney
pilings of the tunnel's arched sides
are gone, the ghosts of windows, they quiet,
their breath chilled and caught, as if death's
cupped hand had squeezed their silly mouths shut.
Blind and dumb, deafened by the procession
of slotted wheels ground into metal tracks,
they are hurled through the earth in cars
heavy as caskets. They can feel the borders
of their bodies recede, their curled insides
dissolve, and when they are little more than warm
pits of fear, the lit ribs of the tunnel
return, the bare stone walls that glide past
the windows, offering their small slabs of light.
Their blank faces emerge luminous, filmed
with sweat, emptied, awed by an inkling
that they might not live forever, hands
folded in their laps, a posture curiously
religious as they are pulled
into the frightening brilliance of the world.

JENNIFER

She sits on the hood of her boyfriend's car,
the wax gone white, ready to be rubbed.
On the door, in the smear, she has written
her name in smooth capitals: *JENNIFER.*
She leans back on the cool windshield, pulls
her suntanned legs to her chest. She pinches
a thigh. Sighs. Twists her hair into a knot
on her head. Three doors down her mother
starts lunch. Her brother jumps, touches
the ceiling. Ten years from now his prints
will still be there. She feels a sharp pain
in her side and bends to it, not knowing
a small pink egg has burst through her ovary,
that it will leave a scar the shape of a baby's
clipped nail. She hopes her dad doesn't
call her in before her boyfriend comes back.
She heard today in school that the world
could end. She can't imagine it. She closes
her eyes and thinks about her boyfriend's
muscles, the soft yellow chamois that will
snap from his hands. She thinks about later
tonight, at the drive-in, how they'll sit
so close in this car, how it will shine.

THE CATCH

The film footage wavers
on the gray TV screen:
fistsfull of Marines flung
from a helicopter, a flower
suspended in air
dropping its bloom of pods.
A row of khakied backs, the square-
shouldered shapes of men, knee-deep
in mud and raising rifles
like fishing rods.
There is the bitter smell of powder,
of too much salt, as bodies,
scooped from a trench, are flopped
like fish on a deck.
Here's what is left
of a boy from Maryland, half a face
and his good right arm. The rest,
scattered on a hillside, his pink
testicles split against
the brain-gray rock. In his breast
pocket, a snapshot, his girl
in a bikini, her whole body sprawled
across the hood of a new Camaro.
She's wet from the blue pool, shining,
car keys dangling from her teeth like minnows.

THE GARDEN

We were talking about poetry.
We were talking about nuclear war.
She said she couldn't write about it
because she couldn't imagine it.
I said it was simple. Imagine
this doorknob is the last thing
you will see in this world.
Imagine you happen to be standing
at the door when you look down, about
to grasp the knob, your fingers
curled toward it, the doorknob old
and black with oil from being turned
so often in your hand, cranky
with rust and grease from the kitchen.
Imagine it happens this quickly, before
you have time to think of anything else;
your kids, your own life, what it will mean.
You reach for the knob and the window
flares white, though you see it only
from the corner of your eye because
you're looking at the knob, intent
on opening the back door to the patch
of sunlight on the porch, that garden
spread below the stairs and the single
tomato you might pick for a salad.
But when the flash comes you haven't
thought that far ahead. It is only
the simple desire to move into the sun
that possesses you. The thought

of the garden, that tomato, would have
come after you had taken the knob
in your hand, just beginning to twist it,
and when the window turns white
you are only about to touch it,
preparing to open the door.

SUNDAY

We sit on the front lawn, an igloo
cooler between us. So hot, the sky
is white. Above gravel rooftops
a spire, a shimmering cross.

You pick up the swollen hose, press
your thick thumb into the silver nozzle.
A fan of water sprays rainbows
over the dying lawn. Hummingbirds

sparkle green. Bellies powdered
with pollen from the bottle-brush tree.
The bells of twelve o'clock.
Our neighbors return from church.

I bow my head as they ease
clean cars into neat garages, file
through screen doors in lace gloves,
white hats, Bible-black suits.

The smell of barbeque rises, hellish
thick and sweet. I envy their weekly
peace of mind. They know
where they're going when they die.

Charcoal fluid cans contract in the sun.
I want to be Catholic. A Jew. Maybe
a Methodist. I want to kneel
for days on rough wood.

Their kids appear in bright shorts,
bathing suits, their rubber thongs
flapping down the hot cement.
They could be anyone's children;

they have God inside their tiny bodies.
My god, look how they float, like birds
through the scissor-scissor-scissor
of lawn sprinklers.

Down the street, a tinny radio bleats.
The sun bulges above our house
like an eye. I don't want to die.
I never want to leave this block.

I envy everything, all of it. I know
it's a sin. I love how you can shift
in your chair, take a deep drink
of gold beer, curl your toes under, and hum.

—*after Wallace Stevens*

ACKNOWLEDGMENTS

Grateful acknowledgment is made to the editors of the following journals and anthologies in which some of these poems, or earlier versions of them, first appeared and/or were reprinted:

Americas Review: "The Catch"
The Beloit Poetry Journal: "Two Pictures of My Sister"
Coydog Review: "China," "Augusta," "Ghosts," and "Jennifer"
Electrum: "The Laundromat" and "The Nurse"
Five Fingers Review: "What My Father Told Me," "Quarter to Six,"
      "Augusta," and "Return"
Poet Lore: "Quarter to Six"
Tendril: "Skipping Stones"
Poetry Flash: "The Catch"
Yellow Silk: "China"
ZYZZYVA: "Sunday," "On the River," "On the Back Porch," and "Ghosts"

"What My Father Told Me" and "Two Pictures of My Sister" were included in *The Courage to Heal: A Guide for Survivors of Child Sexual Abuse* (Harper & Row, 1989); "The Catch," "China," "Ghosts," and "Laundromat" were included in *The Maverick Poets* (Gorilla Press, 1988); "China" was included in *Deep Down: The New Sensual Writings by Women* (Faber and Faber, 1989); "The Twins" was included in *Poet's Voices: Social Issues by Contemporary Poets* (San Diego Poets' Press, 1984); and "Quarter to Six" was included in *The Pushcart Press XI: Best of the Small Presses* (1986).

Some of the poems in this book also were included in *Three West Coast Women* (San Francisco, Five Fingers Poetry, 1987).

I wish to thank the Djerassi Foundation, the MacDowell Colony and The Corporation of Yaddo for fellowships which enabled me to complete this work.

I would also like to express my gratitude to Kim Addonizio, Howard Junker, Steve Kowit, Al Poulin, Ron Salisbury, and my dear friends.

And to Philip Levine, for noticing.

DORIANNE LAUX

Dorianne Laux was born in 1952 in Augusta, Maine and is of Irish, French and Algonquin Indian heritage. Raised in southern California, she barely completed her high school education. Between the ages of 18 and 30 she worked as a gas station manager, sanatorium cook, maid, and donut-holer. A single mother, she took occasional classes and poetry workshops at the local junior college, writing poems during shift breaks. In 1983 she moved to Berkeley, California where she began writing in earnest. Supported by scholarships and grants, she returned to school when her daughter Tristem was 9, and was graduated from Mills College in the Spring of 1988 with a B.A. Degree in English. In 1990 she was awarded a Fellowship in Poetry by the National Endowment for the Arts. *Awake* is her first book of poems.

BOA EDITIONS, LTD.
NEW POETS OF AMERICA SERIES